HBCU PRIDE

HBCU PRIDE

THE TRANSFORMATIONAL POWER OF HISTORICALLY BLACK COLLEGES AND UNIVERSITIES

SHAFEEQ AMEEN, PH.D.

To order additional copies of this book, contact:
Xlibris
844-714-8691
www.Xlibris.com
Orders@Xlibris.com
815747

CONTENTS

DEDICATION

To all the families who understand the cumulative impact of the world we are leaving to our children, don't give up. Life is a journey that has roadblocks, but through the HBCU experience, if you are focused, have clear goals and are willing to embrace change, the outcome will lead you to a destination that is far beyond our ancestors wildest dreams.

ACKNOWLEDGEMENTS

As always, I acknowledge God who has found a way to guide my daily actions and continues to forgive me for my many mistakes. To my parents, Mushin and Frances and my siblings, Runita James and Alvin Muhammad who have provided me with the love, encouragement and the guidance needed to stay true to the content within these pages. To my daughters, Jahaan, Khadijah, Maryam and stepson Jelani Muhammad who are the loves of my life and help keep me motivated in everything I do. Finally, to my wife Kaleema who has been both supportive and understanding since the day we met.

The mother is the first teacher of the child. The message she gives that child, that child gives to the world.

Malcolm X

INTRODUCTION

My college experience has been a long, challenging but life-affirming odyssey. Like the fictional character Odysseus, who returns ten years after the fall of Troy more mature and able to confront all of life's challenges, so too has my odyssey defined me as one forged by the struggles that define many great Americans. This life-changing journey has both molded and shaped me into the man I am today. Being the youngest of an intact African American family, I was blessed with both structure and positive role models. As one of the few families in our neighborhood to have both a mother and father in the same household, I felt blessed. While my father worked, my mother stayed home, took my siblings and I to school, made our lunches every day and waited for us as we arrived home. Our family was balanced, healthy and we all had clearly defined roles. Both my parents came from a religious background in Pittsburgh and South Carolina respectively. Church and Sunday school were mandatory. Because of this fact, I was taught early the difference between right and wrong, a commitment to community service, and respect for my elders. But like many, I was unclear about the path I should follow for my life. I had no immediate or long-term goals to navigate this journey. To this end, college, as it has for so many, became my guide. My college experience served as the place that nurtured my soul and a place where it was safe to fail without fear of abandonment. This beacon of light helped guide a naïve and fragile young man to salvation. Once lost in a sea of uncertainty, I truly felt had a safe place to grow, learn and become the person I was meant to be.

In the fall of 1977, I walked onto my college campus for the very first time. Being raised in a northern urban city, I was amazed at the beauty of the county landscape. The huge white column buildings and opulent spacing were in direct contrast to the clutter and darkness associated with my inner-city experience. Discovering that most Historically Black Colleges and Universities (HBCU's) were built largely to educate the newly freed slaves gave me a sense of pride. I was quickly exposed to many gifted and articulate students determined to make a difference in the world. The professors and administrators were dedicated to our success, and they provided a support system to catch us when we fell. My sense of manhood, academic aspiration, and religion were all shaped during my formative years at this great institution.

HBCU's have not only provided hope and stability to countless numbers of Blacks; they have also contributed greatly to the advancement of America. Until the enactment of the emancipation proclamation, statutes made the teaching reading and writing to slaves was a crime. Freed African Americans were legally barred from higher education and, in many states, from education all together. Historical Black Colleges and Universities bravely took on the task of righting this wrong. Forged by sheer will and self-preservation, African Americans have achieved success at all levels. As a result, some of the most prominent figures in the world matriculated at Black colleges. The list is too long to include all the names, but these are a few: Dr. Martin Luther King, J., Spike Lee, Samuel L. Jackson (Morehouse); Reverend Jesse Jackson & Terrence J. (North Carolina A&T); Nikki Giovanni (Fisk); Thurgood Marshall, Taraji P. Henson, Phylicia Rashad, Debbie Allen, Wendy Raquel Robinson, Anthony Anderson & Sean "Diddy" Combs (Howard); Wanda Sykes (Hampton); Oprah Winfrey (Tennessee State); Erykah Badu (Grambling State); Common (Florida A&M); Kenya Barris (Clark/Atlanta); Rickey Smiley (Alabama State); Brian McKnight (Oakwood); Stephen A. Smith (Winston-Salem State); Lionel Richie (Tuskegee); Reginald Lewis (Virginia State University) and David Banner (Southern). These universities were relevant then and are still relevant today. We must keep them financially sound and academically competitive. There is a common theory that HBCUs have served their usefulness and that African Americans should matriculate at majority White colleges or universities (PWI's). I strongly believe that would be a mistake. Historically Black Colleges and Universities are needed now more than ever.

My individual quest for self-discovery took place at The Virginia State University, a small HBCU in Petersburg, Virginia. It's difficult to put into words, but Virginia State has given me more than I could ever give back. My transformation, the song that echoes in the deepest recesses of my heart, was shaped there. As you turn these pages, let my words resonate and deliver my declaration that the hardest thing in life is a search to find yourself. Here is my journey.

OBSERVATION

"People pay for what they do and still more for what they have allowed themselves to become. And they pay for it very simply; by the lives they lead."

James Baldwin

Why I chose an HBCU?

Sean Combs
Rapper, Producer, Actor, Mogul. Inventor of the Remix
Howard University

It was important for me to go to a school where I would be exposed to new things and meet new people. But I also wanted to be part of a community that understood my life experience. Howard offered all of that and more.

It was my Howard professors who supported my decision to take a once-in-a-lifetime opportunity and work at Uptown MCA Records under the legendary Andre Harrell. The lessons I learned while on campus, and the connections that I made, are part of my life and career every day.

Howard became my family. It gave me a second home. When I couldn't afford a place to live, it was my Howard friends who let me sleep on their floors. It was my Howard family who looked out for me when I didn't have any money for food.

When I started my career in music, many of the people I met at Howard-like Harve Pierre-came with me on my journey.

HBCUs serve a vital role in the African American community, and to that end, the greater community at large. They fill a void that has been lost for many who are seeking a connection to their past and their future. Like other ethnic groups, African Americans try to find purpose in their lives through connections. Without these connections, a vital link to both self and group actualization is missed. The core that is the center of our existence is misaligned; that part that makes us whole is missing. My own individual feelings of belonging can, in part, be traced back to this problem. Like many African Americans, I did not see my own disconnection, but it was there. I'm talking about the place where you know you will always belong. Most ethnic groups call it their place of origin.

Try to visualize this: Italians wandering throughout North America without having the rich and robust history of Italy as their ancestral place of reference, the Irish meandering this land devoid of their vibrant and brazen ancestry, Ireland, or Jamaicans being stripped of the colorful and communal culture of their beloved Jamaica. Well for African Americans, Africa still does not seem like an easy cultural fit. Many Blacks know only America as their place of origin; the continent of Africa seems distant and far removed from their reality. For me, the Black college experience was my starting point to come back home. It was a secure, protective, and familiar place. My HBCU experience provided me with a safe haven from the cruel world which awaited me outside the college campus. I felt like my ancestral parents were welcoming, accepting, and inviting me to come back home. I was surrounded by people who looked like me, had similar backgrounds and who were supportive and nonjudgmental.

According to the National Center for Education Statistics, until the midpoint of the 20th century, more than 90% of African - American students enrolled in higher education in the country were educated at HBCUs. However, since the early 1960's, in part because of public pressures to desegregate higher education, the percentage of African-American college-going students at HBCUs has dramatically declined with only 17% of Black students enrolling in the 101 HBCUs this century. Per the 2018-2019 school year, the National Center for Education Statistics calculated that more than 6,000 fewer students attended the 101 black colleges and universities. The 291,767 totals were down from the 298,134 in the previous year, and was the lowest total since 2001, when there were 289,985 students at historically black colleges. *"There is a distinct possibility that a number of HBCUs could cease to exist in 20 years or so, said Ronnie Bagley, a retired Army Colonel who graduated from Norfolk State University in 1983.*

These colleges and universities have always provided a positive link to our past. Their ability to help shape our future is limitless. As early as 1856, Wilberforce University in Ohio became the first HBCU to be fully owned and operated by African Americans. I beg to differ with critics who believe that the days of Black colleges are numbered. There will always be students, like myself, for whom the Black college experience literally changed the trajectory of our lives. *Over 51 percent of all Black agriculturalists, 50 percent of all Black teachers, 42 percent of all Black physical scientists, 42 percent of all Black biologist, and 35 percent of all Black computer programmers in the United States graduated from an HBCU.* Black colleges have been and continue to be a beacon of light for so many African Americans. Individuals who attend these institutions feel relevant and focused on a society that is not always empathic to the struggles that many Blacks still must overcome. I thank God that I found this source of stability and nurturing at Virginia State University.

Ponder these questions: Why does it seem strange to support and push for the maintenance and growth of historically Black colleges and universities? Does anyone question the utility of Yeshiva University for Jews, the University of Notre Dame for Catholics, or Brigham Young University for Mormons? The answer is a resounding no! This would be unthinkable. Although their doors are open to everyone, these ethically and religiously centric universities cater to a specific population and do so unapologetically. Does anyone ever question their usefulness in the 21st century? America, once the great melting pot now celebrates itself as the nation of inclusiveness and individuality, the salad bowl of the western world. It is essential to define this theory. Why? In a melting pot, individuality is lost, and the dominant ingredient takes over while other ingredients lose significance. Isn't that counterintuitive to a healthy society? Our richness is found in our diversity of thought. I know it sounds like a cliché, but the greatness of a nation is built on its diversity. This is what makes America unique in the world. If one ethnic group sees the power of educating their own, then why is it good for some, but not for all. Isn't that a double standard? I am not saying that it is America's role to understand the disconnectedness of African Americans, but there is so much more we have to offer outside of singing, dancing, and sports. The intellectual power that is housed in HBCUs has been of great benefit to a country that we love.

This is one of the many reasons, HBCUs must remain vital in the 21st century and beyond. Inclusion has its place, but there is always a need for universities like Virginia State, Norfolk State, Hampton, Morehouse, and Spelman, just to name a few. They help preserve the identity for the next generation of leaders. Sometimes, when I relate my experiences at Virginia State University to African American friends and family who went to Predominately White Institutions (PWIs), I see a pain in their eyes. It is clearly registered on their faces a feeling of loss, a sense that they missed out on a piece of their history that can only be experienced through attending and HBCU. Many have told me horror stories of feeling isolated by their peers, not feeling accepted by their professors, and feeling an overall sense of loss at PWIs. Darrell

Dail, a molecular genomics scientist described his feelings attending and HBCU said, *"It was a melting pot of high intelligence and backgrounds. This black diversity made a great playground for great debate and banter. It was truly iron sharpening iron for us all. I wouldn't be the man I am if it weren't for South Carolina State."*

I am not one to believe that there is some covert plan in academia to systematically marginalize African Americans; however, when you are placed in a situation where you are one of only a few in a given group, you can feel uncomfortable. As a part of the university community, this discomfort not only gets magnified but can also go unnoticed. I know it's not the politically correct thing to say, but most people feel more comfortable around individuals who look like them and have similar goals and interest. This is not racist; it's human nature. My Black friends who attended PWIs complained to me about large class sizes, not feeling connected or respected by the professors, administration, or the university community. They felt that they were just being tolerated. Every time the issues of race, poverty, gangs, sports, or rap music came up in class or on campus; they were looked upon as the expert to answer these questions.

Can you imagine routinely being judged on such superficial standards at this level of your educational development? It is disrespectful. Feeling like a stranger in a foreign land is how friends described their experiences at a PWI. I never felt that way at my HBCU and my peers at other HBCUs share the same sentiment. Virginia State University and other historically Black colleges and universities make you feel like family, and families offer unconditional love, support, and guidance, Mind you, Black colleges are not a utopia. Like all families there are arguments and disagreements. For example, some students who attend HBCUs are not academically prepared to be in a college classroom. In addition, many HBCU's need to do a better job keeping their financial books in order before they are forced to close due to mismanagement. Even considering these shortcomings, the positives of attending and HBCU still far outweigh any negatives.

A little history lesson: How soon we forget that it was illegal for African Americans to be taught how to read and write. The fundamental right to an education was denied most of our ancestors. From this inhumane treatment, African Americans learned that true freedom was not breaking away from physical bondage, but as Malcolm said, *"Education is the passport to the future, for tomorrow belongs to those who prepare for it today."* Historically Black colleges and universities were formulated to meet the needs of educating Blacks after the Civil War because they were denied access to White schools. Let us not allow HBCUs to lose their goal of, *Serving the educational needs of Black Americans.* We still need HBCUs because they are our legacy. They link our past to our future and in the process allows us to honor those brave men and women who sacrificed their lives to give us this educational opportunity.

Virginia State University helped to cultivate within me a positive self-identity; in addition, it trained me to set obtainable goals that my HBCU expertly prepared me to achieve. Virginia State taught me that with the right attitude and hard work, you make your own opportunities. *This is illustrated VSU mission statement: The University endeavors to meet the educational needs of students, graduating lifelong learners who are well equipped to serve their communities as informed citizens, globally competitive leaders, and highly effective, ethical professionals.* African Americans can still learn value lessons from this statement. There is still a real fear among some Blacks that after years and years of intellectual brainwashing that they will always be inferior to our White counterparts. Look at how some Blacks lower their voices and eyes around Whites or how they are reluctant to disagree with White even if they are clearly wrong because of fear of retaliation. The reverberating effect of our painful history has had a long and profound impact on the psyche within our community, but attending and HBCU helps dispel these fears and provides those who attend these colleges and universities with a psychological and intellectual confidence that is invaluable.

At HBCUs there are role models who both accessible and willing to assist daily. This is the core foundation of these valuable institutions.

U.S. News & World Report in their Best Colleges Ranking edition annually produces a list of the best colleges and universities in the U.S. Rarely does a HBCU make the list. As African Americans, we must know historically the invaluable contributions Blacks have made to the greatness of this nation without the need of outside recognition. Na'im Akbar, a noted Black psychologist, once said, *"Do what you've got to do to find out who you are, and nobody can stop you."* African Americans should use this approach when presenting the argument to the next generation of scholars why they should attend and HBCU.

At HBCUs, you see both the best and worst within our community. The best manifest itself in academically motivated students who have a vision and the ability to positively contribute to the betterment of our society. Chris, a 2012 graduate of Hampton University, said *"Seeing bright Black people who spoke like me and share a desire to excel was amazing,"* Students like Chris make up a subsection of Blacks who attend these HBCU's. In contrast, students who represent the worst examples are the ones who don't take advantage of the rich opportunities that HBCUs have to offer. These students either don't go to class or severely underperform when they do attend. The transition into college life is never realized. HBCUs are not for everyone, and I completely understand that it is truly a personal choice. However, for many these schools provide the resources that any student could take advantage to be successful. To illustrate that point, in my research the majority of HBCUs are student centered, and the instructors make lessons relevant to the reality of the world in which we live. Students who come to school unprepared academically encounter professors who adjust their methodology to meet the students' individual needs.

In my experience, professors at these schools go well beyond classroom instruction. Routinely, my instructors would see me on campus, pull me aside, sit me down, and talk with me about school and life. They became an extension of my family. I remember my English professor drove me to the local car dealership in Petersburg to get my first car. Situations like these are commonplace at on HBCU campuses. People may argue that this is not the true function of colleges and universities. I would challenge that assumption by showing documented success stories of prominent African Americans who attended HBCUs and flourished because of their enrollment. Iyanu, a 2011 graduate of Florida A&M University said, *"I am proud I attended Florida A&M University (FAMU). It is where I became proud of myself, where I learned to work twice as hard…I liked the fact that my professors understood my struggles and knew how to deal with it. I love the fact that a sea of black folk was busting their butts trying their hardest to get an education."*

The role of historically Black colleges and universities is more than just a place for a formal education. They serve a much higher purpose. HBCUs educate their population for life. The schools mirror the environment that many of these students come from except on a much higher level. On these campuses, you see people who look like your cousin Bobby or your Aunt Nikki. These individuals could have come from your own family. That familiarity helps to smoothly transition students from the comfort of their neighborhoods to the world of academia. Nationally, HBCUs are losing enrollment because Black students are finding more options at PWI's. To help keep the doors open at many of these schools, recruitment of other races is being utilized to boost enrollment. This may not be the intended purpose of HBCUs, but the byproduct of economic necessity is to be inventive. Examples of the changing landscape at HBCUs can be seen in the following colleges and universities; Bluefield State University in West Virginia, currently 82 percent White; Gadsden State Community College in Alabama; currently 71 percent White; Lincoln University in Missouri, currently 60 percent White; and West Virginia State University, currently 50 percent White. These schools whose enrollment were once 100 percent African American are struggling to keep the mission statement of HBCU's true while incorporating strategies to keep the doors opens.

As the image of what it means to be an HBCU is being rescheduled, the spirit and loyalty students attach to these colleges and universities remain strong. HBCUs truly become a part of your family forever. Locally,

I take great pride in recommending Virginia State University and Norfolk State University, two HBCU's that I proudly graduated from, to prospective students. The one thing I say to students contemplating an HBCUs is *if you can't add anything to the college or university don't take anything away from it.* In other words, if you are not going to take advantage of the rich legacy left for you by your ancestors, go somewhere else. From Marian Wright Edelman, founder and Children's Defense Fund, who attended Spelman College in Atlanta, to Dr. Martin Luther King, Jr., Civil Rights Leader, who is a graduate of Morehouse College, every historically black college or university, has produced activists who helped break down the barriers of segregation and transform our nation. On September 13, 2010, President Barack Obama was the keynote speaker at the Urban League Convention during HBCU Week. His topic was on the vital role Black colleges and universities.

President Obama said it best: *"We remember all the men and women who took great risks and made extraordinary sacrifices to ensure that these institutions could exist. We remember that at a critical time in our nation's history, HBCU's waged war against illiteracy and ignorance – and won."*

JOURNEY

---

*"Black people have always been America's
wilderness in search of a promised land."*

Cornel West

Why I chose and HBCU…?

Anthony Anderson - Actor (Black-ish, To Tell the Truth and The Deported)
Howard University

Howard University was the only college I applied to because of the history of their fine arts department. The likes of Debbie Allen, Phylicia Rashad, and Roberta Flack had come through those doors.

I go back and I meet students and I go to homecoming. I talk about how great it is, and I'm like, "Well, you know, there was never really a better time at Howard than when I was there."

I understand that every generation has their time, or whatnot, but we had Puff, we had Amanda Lewis, we had AJ Calloway, we had me, Wendy Raquel Robinson, we had Wendy Davis, we had Carl Anthony Payne, we had Marlon Wayans, we had the group Shai-Taraji P. Henson! And I say, "You look at all people that I have named, and how we've become successful in our own fields, in our own right. Just imagine all that creative energy on the yard at the same time. The hype that you're feeling right now isn't the same as what it was once when we were students there."

And then they understand, they say, "Ok, you may have a point, but you know, Howard's fly as hell right now."

Like fictional character Simba from <u>The Lion King,</u> whose pursuit of self-actualization was long, eventful, and full of suspense, my journey started in the wilderness many Philadelphia natives referred to as *"The Jungle."* In the late 60's and early 70's North Philadelphia was the very definition of urban blithe. Trash, dilapidated homes, and rapid violence were symbolic of the landscape. My family resided in an extremely poor section right off Eric Avenue until I was five years old. At the time, my father was working at the Ford Motors Plant and hated the fact that his family had to live in these conditions.

In North Philadelphia, our family stayed in a small apartment on the second floor. Routinely, my father would come home from working his first job, shower, eat, and prepare to work the evening shift at a local bar. My brother, sister, and I would often complain about seeing mice in the apartment. As the men of the house, when my father was at work, my brother and I took our responsibility to keep our home safe and vermin free seriously. Even though we were charged with this responsibility, the rodents had nothing to fear. I think both my brother and I were more afraid of the mice than they were of us. Because of this fear, the mice were still alive and active when my father returned home from work. Tired and frustrated, he would arrive home and reluctantly kill the mice and throw them outside our bedroom window into a huge dumpster in the alley.

One day my father came home and said, *"I'm not going to let my family live like this anymore. Give me three months, and we will never have to live like this again."* My father was true to his word. Within three months we left the small confines of North Philadelphia to the spacious tree lined neighborhood in the heart of West Oak Lane.

West Oak Lane was like another world. There were fifteen houses on each side of the street. The houses were huge and well-maintained. Each had its own individual lawn and a private garage in the back. All the houses had large porches with a dividing bar to separate one's house from their next-door neighbor, a far cry from the cramped apartment from which we came. Like Moses when he freed the slaves from bondage, our family felt as if our father delivered us to the promise land. On our first night in our new home, I vividly remember my parents sitting us all down after we had finished unpacking. They instructed us to always remember that we were visual examples of how the Whites on our street would perceive Blacks. At the time, I did not understand why my parents felt so adamantly about this, but years later I understand more clearly how perception becomes reality. The way one sees an individual can taint the way one judges an entire group. If we are to be honest, this is not just a Black and White thing, it is a concept universally applied to all races.

One thing that we found out quickly was that we were one of only two Blacks on our street. My next-door neighbor happened to be the other Black family on our block. That's how I met Tonyy. Tonyy was an only child and the product of a divorced family. He lived with his mother, a prominent social worker in the city. His father was a police officer and would visit occasionally on weekends. Tonyy and I quickly became best friends. This may seem strange, but a bonus of being Tonyy's best friend is that I shared in his misfortune. The misfortune of Tonyy being the product of a divorced house turned into a windfall for me because out of guilt, his parents competed in showing him how much they loved him. Anything Tonyy wanted he got. Because I was his best friend, I reaped the benefits of his good fortune. When he went on a vacation, I was invited. When he went out to an expensive restaurant, he would not go unless I was added to the list. Tonyy was my best friend, and I was enjoying all the perks of this relationship.

I entered elementary school in Fall of 1968. I was so excited. During the summer, my mother had purchased new outfits for me, my brother, and sister. As the youngest of three, I did not get the same amount of new clothing. The rule regarding new clothing was understood, I would wear my brother's hand-me-downs once he had outgrown or got tired of them. My brother was larger than me, so often the clothes did not fit, but I appreciated his style and that made the oversized outfits acceptable. My brother loved to dress, and I loved his style. Once a month he would buy a new item to add to his growing wardrobe. During the late 70's and early 80's, the current fad in the inner city was to get your clothes tailor made. Philly has always been known for its own unique style. The look at that time was oversized pants with wide cuffs. During his monthly tailor run, I would travel with my brother to shops where he would bring drawings or have pictures cut out from magazines to show the tailor what style he desired. My brother worked so he could afford this luxury. On the other hand, I was broke and completely depended on the financial generosity of my mother. Unfortunately, she did not view tailor-made clothes a necessity.

During this period, my family moved to a predominately White section of the city. For the first time in my life, I was one of the only Blacks in my class. It's a funny thing; when you are young; the difference in skin colors strangely goes unnoticed. We all sat together in class and played together during recess. Many of my friends in school were White. Our innocence allowed us to see each other as merely human. We never discussed race. The natural state of adolescence lends itself to perpetual bliss when it comes to race relations. I can remember vividly eating together with my White classmates during recess without a care in the world. Honestly, I can say I did not see color. I just enjoyed being a kid. As I grew older, it dawned on me that the only interaction I had with my classmates was at school. I was never invited over to their house. When the school bell rang, our worlds divided, not to be united again until the next school day. I guess this was just an unspoken rule because I never invited my classmates to my house either.

The atmosphere in my elementary classroom was always positive, energetic, and purposeful. My teachers called on me frequently because I had a broad and engaging smile and loved to talk. As the youngest child, you learn quickly to be the center of attention if you ever want to get noticed, as such, I was popular in school. These experiences were consistent throughout my early years in school. I was happy, I enjoyed school, and I loved my family. This idyllic existence all started to dissolve in the Spring of 1971. My neighborhood was slowly starting to change. As Blacks moved in, White residents moved out. My once predominately White elementary school was now heavily populated with Black and Latino students. The social dynamics took a different spin because each culture brought its own social norms. These norms had both positive and negative connotations. On the one hand, it was great being around people who looked like me; on the other hand, I quickly learned that at some point I was going to have to pick what side I was on. No matter which side I selected, there would be consequences based on my decision.

My mother saw the changing tide at both my school and within the neighborhood. She warned my brother and me to be careful. During the early 70's gangs and guns were being introduced into the city. Walking alone or in small groups through different neighborhoods became a dangerous ordeal. Wearing the wrong color could cost you your life. My mother preached the importance of staying focused on our education and cautioned us to avoid associating with the wrong people. This was easier said than done. Both my brother and I were solicited by the local gangs, but thanks to our mother's sage advice and a little bit of luck, we stayed gang free. I struggled to find a way to fit in, and because of this fact, my grades took a nosedive. Quickly realizing I was not meeting the expectations she had set for both my siblings and I; my mother acted. She sacrificed financially and paid for a tutor to help me with my academic issues. Unbeknownst to her, my academic shortcomings had little to do with ability, but rather my lack of desire to be a productive student. My mother valued education, and to this day, she is the head cheerleader in our family when it comes to accumulating degrees. Even though my mother never went to college, she realized early on that education is the true equalizer, affording freedom of choice, financial stability, and respectability within society. Every time my brother, sister, or I would achieve any academic milestone, my mother would proudly tell anyone in shouting distance what accomplishments her children had achieved. Today, she displays that same level of enthusiasm towards her grandchildren, great-grandchildren, nieces, and nephews. One of the reasons I hold a doctoral degree today is because of the educational values my mother instilled in me at an early age. By sheer desire and wisdom that comes with age, my mother has made the pursuit of academic attainment a staple in our family.

Before I get ahead of myself, let me tell you a little about me. I am the youngest of three. I have an older sister by three years, Nita, and an older brother by less than two years, Denny. As a child, I was full of energy. This energy, when left unchecked, was dangerous. I stayed in trouble. I know I drove my mother crazy because there was no rhyme or reason to my outlandish behavior. I was the total opposite of both my siblings who, for the most part, stayed out of trouble. I was always into something. Soon after elementary school, phone calls from teachers became a routine occurrence for my mother. I skipped classes; cut school all together, stole, got into fights, and overall caused mayhem. At the time, I don't think anyone realized that I was just starved for attention. I had the typical youngest child syndrome; lost, confused, and begging for someone to acknowledge my existence. In addition to my many issues, I was academically unmotivated. I lacked social skills and had no clear aspirations for anything besides getting into trouble. My mother gave me as much love and support as she could, but I was still lost. To make matters worse, my parents had recently divorced. My mother was left with both the financial and emotional responsibility of caring for three growing adolescents. This messy situation left me angry and resentful of my father for leaving my mother, my siblings, and I in this unstable condition. As a last-ditch effort to grab hold of anything that could give me stability, I turned to my brother. I looked to him to help fill the void left by my father's absence. He tried to fill the gap, but with less than two years difference between us, he had his own issues to contend with and as such was a limited in the support that I needed at the time. Nonetheless, like many fatherless households, as the oldest male he now had the inevitable task of being the father, brother, and male role model in our home. Looking back, I never realized how hard it must have been for him.

Toward the end of my senior year, right before graduation, my mother asked me what my plans were after high school. This is probably a question that I should have asked myself and for which I should have had an answer years earlier. As you can imagine, I didn't have a clue. I had not applied to any colleges and even if I did, I didn't know what I wanted to pursue as a career. Fortunately for me, my mother had already been successful in sending both my sister and brother to school, so she had already formulated a plan of action. I can still remember that fateful day. My mother woke me up early and told me we were going to the college recruitment center. The center was in downtown Philadelphia and specialized in matching students with colleges that best fit their academic needs. As we walked through the oval doors, my mother said loudly, *"My baby going to college."* I could see a faint tear rolling down her cheek. I'm not sure if she was happy that *"her baby"* was going to college or was just overjoyed to get her last and most challenging child out the house. Knowing mom, it was probably a little bit of both. At the center, the recruiter looked over my SAT scores and my high school transcript and shook his head. Neither of the two items was very impressive. After taking a deep breath, he asked me what college or colleges I was considering. He did this out of a matter of politeness because my academic shortcoming severely limited my choices. Boldly, I proclaimed that I wanted to go to the University of Hawaii. My mother turned to me with that look that only a mother can give a child and said emphatically, *"Boy, are you crazy?"* Trying hard but unsuccessfully to maintain himself and hold back laughter, the recruiter first turned to me and then my mother. I think I left him speechless. Why did I say the University of Hawaii? I'm still not sure. Maybe it was because I always wanted to visit Hawaii, and, in my adolescent mind, it made sense. At that point, my mother took control of the entire situation as it was obvious that I was out of my depth and quickly sinking. She asked the recruiter which school I could realistically get into. He searched his database for what seemed like an eternity and finally said he had two schools that could accept me. I wasn't sure what he meant by that because I was still dreaming of palm trees and laying on the sands of Maui. Both schools that he suggested were small and historically Black. One was Voorhees University in Denmark, South Carolina, and the other was Virginia State University in Petersburg, Virginia. You know in life how some moments are crystal clear and others a blur? Well, after that moment, I can't tell you what transpired for the next few days. All I know is that within a week, I was headed down I-95 to Petersburg, Virginia. My life as an HBCU student had just begun!

> *"As long as we are not ourselves, we will try to be what other people are."*
>
> Malidoma Patrice

Why I chose an HBCU...?

Stephen A. Smith, Sports Journalist and Television Personality (ESPN2's First Take)
Winston-Salem State University

I was in a critical persuasive writing class, and the professor for the class was the editorial page editor for the *Winston-Salem Journal*. He read an essay of mine and said, "You are a natural born sport writer. Let's go out to lunch." He took me straight to the *Winston-Salem Journal* and introduced me to the sport editor, who hired me on the spot as a clerk.

My career just essentially went from there. The guys that I worked with on the copydesk were all white, and they were fantastic to me. They treated me like family and literally taught me the business. How to write, how to go about pursuing a story.

One day the sports editor, Terry Oberle, asked me to write a feature about Wake Forest soccer, which was ranked No. 3 in the nation. I had never watched a game of soccer in my life. I walked up to the coach and I said to him, "I know nothing about soccer whatsoever, but I want to be a sportswriter. Is there anything you can do to help me?" …He called the whole team over, and he said, "Give him complete, unadulterated access to the next three days. Whatever he wants, give it to him." The coach taught me the game…over the next three days. I wrote a two-page feature and the sports desk ran it in the Sunday paper. Terry called me into his office that Monday and said, "Congratulations, you're the new lead writer for the Wake Forest soccer team."

Prior to enrolling at Virginia State University, I had my first exposure to the Black college experience through my sister. She attended Johnson C. Smith University, a historical Black college in Charlotte, North Carolina. At the time, I was a senior at Olney High School in Philadelphia. Upon my freshmen year at Olney, the school was four years into forced integration. Olney had been all white, but due to a nationwide mandate on the integration of all public school, little Black kids from the other side of the town were bussed in. My brother, sister, and I were products of the first, second, and third wave of minority students brought to Olney. Olney was about a thirty-five-minute commute from West Oak Lane, but it felt like the other side of the world. These were not the same White kids I had befriended in elementary school. They were bigger, meaner, and quick to let Black students know they were unwelcomed. Due to this experience, I was thrust into a cultural juggernaut, and fortunately for me, I was ready to breathe in everything it had to offer.

My mother had recently remarried. A strong Black woman, she had for some time managed to primarily raise three children on her own. At the time, both my sister and brother were away at college and I God willing, was soon to follow. As a result of me having one foot out the door, this new man in the house did not faze me. Because I had grown accustomed to not seeing my biological father, I felt comfortable with my mother's new partner. I was blessed with the ability to not hold grudges, so with the man my mother had chosen to play the paternal role of father in the house, I never took it as an affront to my dad. If her new man helped pay the bills and provided my mother a level of comfort, I was cool. My stepfather was named Al. Per my mother's insistence, we were instructed to call him Mr. Al as a sign of respect. My mother was old-school, and she was big on raising respectful children. Mr. Al was a bus driver for the Southeastern Pennsylvania Transportation Authority (SEPTA). I liked Mr. Al. To my delight, he never attempted to take on the role of father. Mr. Al was short, and I'm sure he was tested because of his lack of height. Due to this fact, he had what experts categorize as a Napoleon Complex. The layman's definition of a Napoleon Complex is a short man who hates the world because of his height. To express his displeasure, he becomes overly mean and aggressive. He is always ready to prove to the world he is not going to take shit from anyone. Mr. Al fit this description perfectly. He had a gun and a bat and was not afraid to use either. Nonetheless, he always treated me with respect and my mom seemed to like him. To get a clear picture of Mr. Al, just think of George Jefferson from *"The Jefferson's"* the sitcom that aired from the mid-70's to the mid-80's. He even had some of his same mannerisms, mostly the swag.

On my first college trip, Mr. Al and my mom took the family to my sister's graduation. The trip from Philadelphia to Charlotte was long, but I was so excited partly because I could drive on the highway for the very first time. I was a little scared, but ready for a new adventure. As I mentioned earlier, the drive was long, exceptionally long. I didn't know the state of North Carolina was so large. Once we arrived at the university, I realized that the trip was well worth the ride. Seeing all the Black faces, I was filled with wonderment. I had never seen so many young Black people carrying book bags and brief cases in my entire life. I felt so proud because these brothers and sisters looked serious, like they were on a mission. Now if that wasn't enough, when I gazed upon those Nubian sisters, I thought, "Oh my God! These sisters are glorious!" Maybe it was the long drive, but the sight of these Nubian queens had me feeling dizzy. I felt like I was ready to drop to the ground. "Man! If this is what a historically Black college looked like, sign me up!"

My sister took us all on a tour of her campus. It was small but full of activity. She introduced us to her friends. I could hear her friends whispering to her, "He's so cute." At least that is what I thought I heard. As the evening approached, we went back to the hotel and changed. My sister said there was a party off campus and that my brother and I were invited. What? And HBCU party! I played it cool, but I was struggling to contain my excitement. Even though the party officially started at 10 PM, but by 7PM I was already dressed and smelling good. This was my first college party, and I was determined to make the experience memorable. I can still recall the evening as if it were yesterday. We left the hotel, and I saturated my body with about a half bottle of cologne. As I walked to the car, I started practicing my dance moves. The car ride seemed like it took forever. Once we arrived, I could feel the sweat on my palms, but my confidence was high. As we approached the front door, I played out in my head everything I was going to say and do. I was ready. As soon my sister opened the front door, all I heard booming into the atmosphere were the lyrics to "Ring My Bell," a popular dance tune in the late 70's by Anita Ward, as groups of college students were dancing and enjoying the music. My confidence must have escaped me because throughout the night, I did not dance once. I was a wallflower, dying in the corner. Even though my reality did not live up to my expectations, I will never forget that night at my first HBCU party.

"My experiences at Princeton have made me far more aware of my 'Blackness' than ever before. I have found that at Princeton, no matter how liberal and open-minded some of my White professors and classmates try to be toward me, I sometimes feel like a visitor on campus as if I really don't belong."

Michelle Obama

Why I chose an HBCU…?

Lionel Richie, legendary top-selling R&B singer, songwriter, and musician.
Tuskegee University

I was born and raised on Tuskegee University's campus. It was probably one of the greatest things that ever happened to me in my life. All the things that Black America stands for today were built into my growing up. It was a part of the lesson plan.

It was one of the returns to Tuskegee and to attend the university. Going to that school gave me the confidence of basically knowing who I am and where I am in this great big world that we live in. I think the part that I loved the most was who came through Tuskegee at that time. We had some of the greatest leaders and

controversial subjects of our time. From Malcolm X to Martin Luther King, Jr. to H. Rap Brown to Stokely Carmichael to Odetta to Hugh Masekela, the Temptation to James Brown and every other wonderful artist. It was just a cultural mecca.

It was just one of those wonderful times in history when everyone would come through. Not to mention the fact that I was born and raised in and around the Tuskegee Airmen. The community and the environment-it just raised me. It raised me to who I am today.

Although my first college experience left an indelibly positive imprint on my mind, I had a totally different experience when I went to visit my brother at his university. My brother attended West Chester University, a Predominately White Institution (PWI) in West Chester, Pennsylvania. Throughout my childhood and lasting well into my adult life, my brother has been my role model. Only being a few years apart in age, we had similar interests and viewed life in roughly the same way. When he selected a local university to attend, I knew he would still play a major part in my life. Occasionally, I would travel to West Chester by bus, about a 45-minute ride from Philadelphia, and stay with him and his roommates in their off-campus apartment. This was an important time for me because I was able to see the college experience up close and personal. My brother would take me to the campus and introduce me to his friends.

One thing that I soon noticed was that the Black students on campus appeared isolated from the White's. Like a dysfunctional marriage, these two cultures lived side-by-side but did not walk together or even interact with each other on campus. This didn't seem completely strange because I had experienced the separation among races before, but having seen the unity on my sister's campus, I was taken aback. I naively, thought the world of academia would erase these petty differences. As my brother and I would walk throughout the campus, some Whites would cut their eyes as if to say, "why are you here?" The feeling of togetherness I saw at my sister's HBCU was completely absent at West

Chester. Each time I would visit was reminiscent of those occasions when I would walk through Nordstrom's with a hoodie on; suspicious eyes were always on me. This is how I felt at West Chester University. Listening to my brother tell me about his negative experiences at the university, he felt the same way as me every day. He expressed that Blacks had to choose either forced assimilation or total isolation. There was no middle ground. As a result, I began to see a change in the attitudes of both my brother and his friends as assimilation wasn't a choice, they felt comfortable with. Both he and his friends were becoming increasingly more militant and race conscious. My brother's conversations began to include phrases like "us versus them." Walking around campus and having candid conversations with my brother began to become awkward. The brother that I knew and loved, along with his friends, appeared unusually guarded. Feeling out of place and unwanted will do that to you.

Just like my sister and I, my brother's college experience shaped his perception of both himself and the world in which he lived. To this day, he is much more militant than either my sister or me. I remember my brother relating stories of cross burnings on the front lawn of his campus; difficulty in renting apartments off-campus because of the color of his skin; and being ridiculed by professors, administrators, and fellow students because of his race. I have heard similar stories of African Americans feeling alienated on the campuses of PWIs. One body of research measured the impact of alienation experienced by Black students. The measuring tool was the University Alienation Scale. In over 20 years of testing, Black students consistently scored significantly higher on the alienation scales than White students and generally higher than other minority groups such as Hispanics and Asian Americans. Those results were consistent in tests done on the East and West Coast and on northern and southern campuses (Bennett; D'Augelli; & Fleming, 2011).

My brother would often bemoan his college choice and would readily express that if he had to do it all over again, he would select and

HBCU. His natural maturation and development as a man and even as an American was negatively impacted by his college experience. In my observation, college is a self-fulfilling prophecy for those who are observant: Collective experiences you bring to school become heightened through your exposure. In contrast, for many African Americans, the Black college experience teaches you to view school as a building block, a process. You learn that the aim of education is to teach you how to think. Once you digest this concept, life becomes much more manageable. Professors at HBCUs often promote the idea that thinking is critical to succeeding in life. One thing I often tell young people contemplating higher education is that college operates differently from a trade school. The thinking man (or woman) realizes the difference quickly. While trade schools are great institutions of learning, most traditionally focus primarily on how to do something. The thinker plans, organizes, and follows through. This requires the ability to think much more critically. In my experience, at Black colleges, instilling the universal concept of preparing global thinkers prepared to tackle the challenges of the 21st century and beyond is embedded in the mission statement. I know that my brother's college experience had a profound negative impact on him, and he is haunted by that decision even to this day. In contrast, HBCUs shields its students from this fate by offering unconditional love and continual support.

While watching CNN one evening, I saw a small piece done on the unrest at Yale University. African American students were angered over White students' dressing in blackface during Halloween. This was one of several controversial incidences taking place at a PWI, and I imagined just one of many aspects of campus life that made Black students feel both devalued and disrespected at Yale. A 2014 study conducted by researchers at New York University, Columbia University, and the University of Pennsylvania found that when students contacted professors for mentorship, faculty were significantly more responsive to White men than women and people of color, particularly in private universities. To make a problematic situation even worse, faculty often single out students for their race during conversations in and outside of class. Further, according to a 2013 Association for the Study of Higher Education paper, which conducted focus groups with graduate students at seven universities, students of color reported many instances of faculty suggestion their race affected their interest. One participant named Jasmine, a Black student studying computer science, said her professor referred to her as *"one of you. You've never taught a student before? Never taught a softball player?" the students recounted"* [I was] trying to figure out what he meant by, *'one of you.'* And he finally came out and said, *"I've never had a Black student before."* It was just extremely uncomfortable. The former president of the University of Missouri was accused of failing to act after a string of racist behaviors, such as the African American student association president being harassed by men in a pickup truck yelling racial slurs during the rehearsal of a school play, and the drawing of a swastika with feces in one of the college's bathrooms. The president resigned in November of 2016 after widespread student protests calling for him to quit. In summary, these incidents further highlight the need for African American students to consider the impact that an HBCU could have on both their academic and social well-being.

"Not everything that is faced can be changed, but nothing can be changed until it is faced."

James Baldwin

Why I chose an HBCU…?

Terrence J, Actor and Television Personality (*E! News & Think Like a Man*)
North Carolina A&T

I was not the best student in high school. I had poor grades, and so when I was applying to a lot of other colleges, I didn't get accepted. North Carolina A&T, they took a change on me.

Pretty much everything that I went through in school helped to prepare me for my career. A lot of the business relationship that I have now-Steve Harvey, Shaquille O'Neal-they've all members of the fraternity, Omega Psi Phi, that I became a part of when I was at A&T. All the public speaking that I had to do there, as a student body president, helps me now with all the speaking I have to do when I'm on TV or I'm hosting an event.

It was a transformative experience. Between when I entered at 17, 18 years old, and when I graduated, I became a new man. And that's why I think HBCU's are so important. For a kid like me, it gave me a chance, and I wouldn't be where I am today if they didn't take a chance on me.

"Nigger, get that pork out of this house." Those were the first words I heard from my college roommate. His name was Ray, and, like me, Ray was from Philadelphia, but one of the major differences between Ray and me was that he was from the hood. Ray grew up in one of the roughest housing projects in North Philadelphia (Richard Allen) while I, on the other hand, was raised in West Oak Lane. In the late 60's and 70's, West Oak Lane was a quasi-suburban neighborhood, sadly today is has fallen into urban blithe. Ray and I both were entering our freshmen year at Virginia State. The comment Ray made about pork centered on mother placing two pounds of bacon in the refrigerator of our new off-campus apartment on West Washington Avenue in Petersburg, Virginia. You must understand that up to that point in my life, bacon was my favorite meal. I say meal because I could eat it for breakfast, lunch, and dinner. For me, if it was time to eat, bacon was on the menu. I have since developed a more sophisticated pallet.

Being raised in North Philadelphia around a lot of Muslims, Ray, like many northerners, had been influenced by the Islamic dietary habits. Keep in mind, I didn't really know Ray; the college had placed us together because we both needed housing and all available space on campus for the fall semester had been taken) and also because we were both from Philadelphia. Even though Ray and I were from the same city, we were from two totally different worlds; our backgrounds could not have been more dissimilar. I had, at that point, lived a quiet and sheltered life; by contrast, Ray had been exposed and harden by the unforgiven inner-city streets. He had developed a toughness that, even to this day, I do not possess.

Upon our first introduction, Ray requested, no demanded I call him Chop. I thought the name sounded stupid, but that was his preference. Frankly, as a young man entering the world of academia, I did not think addressing my roommate as Chop in public matched my new level of sophistication. The comment remained in my head, but it did not escape from my lips. My comments were like thought bubbles flowing outside my head without making a sound. The reason this was a completely internal dialog is that if I would have expressed this to Ray; sorry I mean Chop; he would have kicked me ass. I had one fight prior to entering Virginia State and I got knocked out. I was zero and one and I wasn't about to go zero and two. One day, very politely I did get up the nerve to ask him, "Why do they call you Chop?" He reached up to his lips, open his mouth, and pulled out four partial teeth. This was both disgusting and as I learned later, predictable behavior for my roommate.

Chop graduated from Benjamin Franklin High School in North Philadelphia. Life for him evolved around basketball first, girls second, getting high third and academics was a distant fourth. Our first month on campus, Chop was on the basketball court more than he was in class. His goal was to be a walk-on at Virginia State and parlay that into a basketball scholarship and eventually make it to the NBA. Chop missed the part where you had to keep at least a 2.0 grade point average to begin this process. I must admit, he was talented. I loved watching Chop play because he'd score and talk shit all the way to the other end of the court. He loved talking shit. This was Philadelphia basketball 101. Players from Philly were known for being gritty, toughminded, and loose with their lips. One of my many highlights at Virginia State was a pick-up game we had on campus over the summer. I could play a little, but CHOP WAS THE BALLER. Moses Malone was in town for the weekend. Yes, that Moses Malone, the future Hall of Famer. At the time, he was a member of the Houston Rockets. He attended Petersburg High School High and was one of the first players to successful go straight from high school to the pros. As we assembled the teams, it was Chop and I, along with three other Virginia State students. Moses and a group of locals from Petersburg were our opponents. They crushed us, and Moses Malone showed no mercy. He shoved, pushed, and dunked every time he got the ball (which was often). I'm not sure if anyone else on his team even scored. He must have forgotten we were a bunch of college freshman just trying to have a little fun. Chop took both the game and loss seriously. I think he thought Moses was going help him get into the NBA.

I spent two years with Chop at Virginia State, including the one semester off-campus. Both Chop and I found housing in the spring of 1978 and lived next door to each other in Williams Hall the freshmen dormitory. I enjoyed spending time with Chop because he brought me out of my shell and acted more like a brother than a friend. After our sophomore year, I didn't see Chop again on campus. Some people told me he dropped out; others said he was kicked out. In any case, I enjoyed my friendship with Chop, and I wish him all the best.

Sometimes, growing up in a major city affords you a level of aggression that does not come as easy for someone who is raised in a small town. My attitude coming to Petersburg was like that. Even though I had grown up in a middle-class section of Philadelphia, I felt a level of superiority over my southern counterparts. This false sense of superiority was both unwarranted and undeserved. After years of soul searching and having experiences with people throughout the country, I have come to realize that, in many way, being raised in a small town places individuals in a more humane environment, allowing them to see the world from a different perspective. I can only imagine how refreshing and enlightening it would have been to see life without having on blinders, being totally unguarded in my interactions with people. As I would hear my southern friends on campus talk about leaving their front doors open for family and friends to come and go at will, how neighborhood when their parents were away or at work, it sounded foreign to me. This may have happened in the north, but I surely never saw it. In the south, the community became the extended family, and as a northerner, I just couldn't relate to that reality. The lack of material items in the south forced children, out of necessity, to be creative and learn that some things in life you could do without. I became more envious, seeing how simplicity allows the world to move at a much slower pace; being away from the city taught me how the simpler things in life seem to be more rewarding. In the north, it appeared to me that life was a battle just to survive and only your family seemed to look out for your best interest. The concept of southern living was beginning to cause a change in how I viewed the world. My HBCU helped me appreciate the tapestry of southern living and how valuable that communal life is to one's well-being.

Initially, I had a negative view of the south, and felt that the atmosphere and the environment were backwards to that of the so-called progressive north. I saw the south through distorted lens. As the grey has begun to dominate my beard, I have found renewed respect for the south and the jewels that it has produced. The south's reverence for family, commitment to God, and respect for the past have become very appealing as I grow older. African Americans will always be historically linked to the south, for better or worse. This was one of my HBCU self-discoveries.

SELF-DISCOVERY

"Defining myself, as opposed to being defined by others, is one of the most difficult challenges I face."

Carol Moseley-Braun

Why I chose an HBCU…?

David Banner, Rapper, Producer (*Lil Wayne*), and Actor (*The Butler*)
Southern University

Being Southern's SGA president taught me something. It showed me that you can do something right. That was the first time in my life that I did something all the way right and didn't cut any corners, taking advantage of the position. I worked every day eight hours a day in the office. It gave me a microcosm of what my life was going to be…"

On a rainy night in the Fall of 1979, I was blessed to hear the Black revolutionary icon Kwame Ture (formerly Stokely Carmichael). Kwame Ture, of Trinidadian-American decent became a prominent figure in both the Civil Rights and global Pan-African Movements. He changed his name in 1978 to honor Kwane Nkrumah and Ahmed Sekious Toure, two African Socialist leaders who had befriended him when he relocated to Africa. This Black icon grew up in the United States where he became a social activist while attending Howard University.

Kwame Ture was the keynote speaker at Virginia State University during the monthly Eminent Scholar's Series on campus. His three books, *Ready for Revolution, Stokely Speaks,* and *Black Power: The Politics of Liberation* are classic pieces of literature that have become hallmarks in the Pan African Movement. Mr. Ture lectured to a captive audience about the need to be visionaries and to devote one's life to the struggles of Black people. He urged the students to look within and to find out what positive contributions they could make to society in general and to Black people specifically. His words seemed to be directed at me. Still in a state of social and intellectual development, I was ready for a change. I didn't know it at the time, but this was one of my purposes for being at Virginia State University. I would never have received this introduction into the Pan African Movement at a PWI.

The message of empowerment and commitment to social justice motived both my classmates and I to strive for something greater than any of us could have imagined at the time. Through Mr. Ture, we saw a fellow HBCU attendee who was focused and determined. He stood tall and regal in a red, black, and green robe that was a symbol of pride and honor to our impressionable eyes. His words dripped like honey out of his mouth. He was someone who not only spoke about struggle but who also lived that struggle every day and was willing to sacrifice his life for the liberation of his people. One of my favorite quotes of his was, *"There is a higher law than the law of government. That's the law of conscience."* This quote is so relevant to what is occurring in countless cities throughout the US and aboard as people of all races are protesting for basic human right of African Americans.

Throughout the lecture, he urged the audience to stand up for justice at any cost. He peppered his words with references from the Civil Rights Era and the newly formed Pan African Movement. Mr. Ture said that we had to fight apathy, and that the only barrier to our success was us. He chronicled his life, highlighting his emerging activism in high school, his rejection of scholarships to prestigious White universities, becoming a Freedom Rider during his freshman year at Howard, his multiple arrests, and his decision to leave the United States, abandon the non-violent stance of the Civil Rights Movement and pick up the mantel of Pan-Africanism in Guiana. He continued throughout his speech to preach about racial pride and our obligation as HBCU students to honor the ancestors who sacrificed so much for us to be here today. He repeatedly cautioned us to never forget that a price had been paid for us to be able to attend this university. Mr. Ture was not only speaking of a financial cost, but also a physical one as well. *Your ancestors cry out for you, he said. Their dreams are your future-never forget it.*

Like many young African Americans, sad to say, this was the very first lecture I had ever attended. I never imagined that I could be patient enough to sit attentively for hours and listen to someone speak about issues of sacrifice, serving others, and having a commitment to social justice. I was so moved that even after thirty years, I get chills remembering the impact he had on me and my friends that evening. This speech was my baptism into the Black college experience. Place me in the water because I was ready to be saved. Mr. Ture was the one who coined the phrase "Black Power." This realization helped me envision the true power of attending a HBCU. Even though I was excited, I was somewhat afraid that in such a short time, college was exposing me to feelings and emotions that I had never felt before. For the first time, I realized the magnitude of this undertaking, and I was scared. Was college becoming more than I had bargained for? I soon was going to find out.

Was I capable of growing academically? Did I have the ability? Was it too late? These were questions that ran through my mind during my first two years at Virginia State. As a result of my academic apathy in high school, I felt ill-prepared for the rigors of college life. Up to that point, I had not taken education seriously, and for the first time I felt ashamed. During my formative years, my mother routinely pushed me to work harder and study. She would encourage me to strive to be my best, but her encouragement mostly fell on deaf ears. I vividly remember during his speech Mr. Ture saying, *"Frederick Douglas said that the youth should fight to be leaders today... We must begin to start building those institutions and to fight to articulate our position, to fight to be able to control our universities..."* After hearing Mr. Ture's powerful words, I felt compelled to reevaluate my priorities. This was my introduction into life beyond my narrowly constructed walls of ignorance. One of the many benefits of attending a HBCU is that the schools give so many African Americans a new start. They provide an outlet for some individuals who need redemption from their prior sins of mediocrity. HBCUs furnish many wayward souls with direction, one-on-one attention, and compassion. In my experience, the small class sizes and the individualized instruction are like a high school setting only on a higher academic level. HBCUs were founded on the premise that if no other schools of higher learning would accept us, we could and would educate our own. Many may argue, and rightfully so, that college is not designed to be a tutorial center. However, if this is the avenue that some of us venture down then, as Billie Holliday sang in her soulful sagacious style, *"God bless the child who's got his own."* There will always be students who fall through the cracks at PWIs. In my analysis, while this does not apply to all students, HBCUs can be the safety net for those whom need that added support.

Why I chose an HBCU…?

Rickey Smiley, Comedian (*The Rickey Smiley Show, Dish Nation & Rickey Smiley for Real*)
Alabama State University

You go to a Black college; you're really going to learn a lot about your culture. You're going to have an appreciation for the people that came before you because those professors are not going to let you forget where you came from. At some schools you might be just a number, but I know at Alabama State, and different HBCU's, teachers know you by name, and you have a relationship with these teachers. I absolutely love Alabama State. But I love Alabama A&M as well, even though Alabama A&M is our main competition, because A&M was the first college to put me up on stage and pay me to perform. They would book me for homecoming; I would jump in my '77 Cutlass and drive over to Huntsville with some friends. I remember my first check. I got maybe $400. I'll never

forget it. That was a lot...that was like four grand now. Talking about '89, '90, $400 is like four grand. You can do a lot with that!

There was a tradition at Virginia State University in the spring of every year: the annual Pool Party. This was an event not to be missed. One of Greek letter organizations (a fraternity or sorority) would sponsor the party. The Delta's (Delta Sigma Theta) and the Ques (Omega Psi Phi) were famous for giving the best jams. The pool was situated inside of Daniels Gymnasium. Music would be pumped into the pool, and sounds could be heard throughout the entire campus. There were one of two things you could do: sit in the bleachers and watch from afar or get in the water and enjoy yourself. Well, being skinny, shy, and devoid of any rhythm, I was not about to get in the water. One of the benefits of staying in the bleachers was that you could play the dozens and joke everyone who ventured into the pool. The only drawback was that you were only a spectator, and anyone who got in the water was having fun. It was like taking your sister to the prom-she is technically a female, but it defeats the purpose of the event.

The pool party was held at the very end of finals week. The purpose was to relieve the stress from all the exams. Chuck Brown and the Soul Searchers, a Washington, D.C. Go-Band, had the number one hit on Black college campuses during this period. The song was called, *"Da Butt."* Spike Lee popularized this song in his movie <u>School Daze</u>. As the sounds blasted from the speakers, the excitement generated in the water became electrifying. The rhythm of the music and the motion of black bodies in the water, conjured up in my mind the tribal dances of our ancestors. This sight was enough to make a brother want to get into the water regardless of his limitations. I wished I had the nerve to get in, but neither my bleacher mates nor I had developed enough confidence. My lack of rhythm and my one hundred and twenty pounds made my decision easy. It was too early in my college career to subject myself to that much humiliation. Therefore, instead of being wet and embarrassed, I played the dozens on everyone in the water as I secretly consoled myself with the thought, *"My day would come."*

Before the luxury of having multiple venues to eat on campus, there was Jones Dining Hall aka the school cafeteria. This was the only game in town. They served three meals: breakfast, lunch, and dinner. If you missed any of these and didn't have money to go shopping at the local supermarket, grocery store, or fast food restaurant you had to wait to the next day to eat. This made the daily ritual of going to the school cafeteria always interesting. Some days were so slow that the only topics of conversation were the bad food and being broke, but on other days, excitement filled the air. For example, a simple discussion about someone's cafeteria attire could lead to a full-scale confrontation. This confrontation could occasionally escalate into a *"food fight."* Now keep in mind the movie *Animal House*, an embellishment of the white college experience, had recently been released with the infamous food fight scene in the cafeteria. I imagine in some small measure it affected college campuses throughout the US-yes, even HBCU's.

The *"food fights"* would usually begin with one of the fraternities, social organizations, or the football team getting loud and then tossing food at someone. A hamburger would sail across a row of tables, and it would be quickly followed by French fries and then dessert. In a matter of seconds, the quiet cafeteria became a battle zone. The girls who thought they were cute would be the first victims. The content of the food and the severity of the damage depended on the time of day. Most food fights occurred either during lunch or dinner. Exam week was a prime time for this mayhem because everyone was stressed and needed some form of relief. When food began to fly, the best move was to duck under the table until the campus police were called. On rare occasions, a fight would break out because someone didn't appreciate having their clothes decorated with ketchup and mustard. For the most part, it was simply good, clean fun. Let us just say it was an exercise in elementary civil disobedience. With final exams in session, both comic and physical relief was needed to combat the academic pressure of college life. As a result of *"food fights,"* the daily routine of high stakes exams was temporarily interrupted.

Don't get me wrong, there weren't always food fights and pool parties; there was also class. In high school, I never developed a study habit because as the words clearly implies, you must study and make a habit of it. I did neither. My approach to studying was to wait until the day before the exam and cram. This didn't work in high school and it definitely didn't work in college. I brought that same lackadaisical attitude to college, and I suffered greatly because of it. I soon found out that I was not alone. My academic advisor, Dr. William Wyatt, told me that HBCU's provided Black students an opportunity that White colleges would not. He stated that the opportunity of admission was a gift that some, not all, took for granted. In addition, he mentioned that there would be a percentage of my peers who would drop out and waste this gift. They would not see the vision and the dream that their ancestors fought had for them to attain would never be realized. He further stated that some students would be forced to face the grim reality of returning home without a college degree and in addition have to explain to family and friends that they had either dropped out or been kicked out of school. Those who came to school for the wrong reasons or individuals who felt that because it was and HBCU that it was inferior academically and they did not need to study, fell into these categories. My roommate, Chop, and several of my friends were victims of this scenario.

Many Blacks fall into the trap of being their own worst enemy. They expect less academically of Black colleges because *"we are in charge."* This is the slave mentality! Dr. Wyatt would often warn me of this fact. How can Blacks ever expect to be respected as an educated people if we continue to hold on to this fatalistic mindset? It took a while, but I promised myself that my college experience would not be wasted. As I grew both politically and academically, I learned to treasure both the gift and opportunity that Virginia State and all HBCU's provide. When my advisor spoke of those individuals who would give up or were kicked out of school, at the time, I did not realize how right he was. I started to notice my classmates who partied and skipped classes throughout the school year would not return after the winter or summer breaks.

During my first two years, I was starting to fall victim to the exact same scenario my advisor warned me about. For example, during my first two semesters at Virginia State, I remember taking several morning classes. My morning classes started at 8AM. Why I took morning was pure stupidity on my part because I am not a morning person. I found myself missing at least three classes a week. That was a recipe for disaster. After a month, I stop going to class all together. By the end of my second semester, my GPA (grade point average) was so low I owed the school points. I gave Virginia State every reason to put me out. Instead they put me on academic probation, assigned me a tutor and provided me the support I needed to be successful. Thank God Virginia State never gave up on me!

I was *"blessed,"* and I mean truly blessed, to take the opportunity and assistance Virginia State provide and change my way before it was too late. My HBCU and my life quickly mirrored each other becoming intertwined. I am not trying to sound new age, but I had become utterly lost to the point where I did not know who I was or where I was going with my life. Virginia State university became my light. The University gave me guidance, confidence, and a safe place to develop into the person I was soon to become. If it were not for that light, I would never have survived my college experience. Many of my HBCU peers echo these same sentiments when we discuss the impact that our schools have made on our lives. Please don't misunderstand me, there were many students who arrived at Virginia State University and other HBCU's throughout the United States with excellent academic resumes: valedictorians of their senior classes, student council presidents, true scholars, who had a vision and a plan prior to them ever stepping foot on to campus. These are not the individuals I am addressing. My focal point is to shed light on the marginal-the student that needed that extra pat on the back, a guiding hand, and in some cases a kick in the butt. The reason I emphasize these points is that this was my experience. One thing that makes my story unique is the fact that it affected me so profoundly that I felt obligated to tell others. I would feel like a failure if I did not communicate my journey. I would feel like I let my fellow

HBCU peers down if I did not proclaim proudly the debt, I owe to Virginia State University and the debt my peer owes to their HBCUs.

One of the greatest pleasures of college life was meeting students from different cities and states. During my freshman year, I met Wayne. Wayne was from Brooklyn, New York. He and I bonded from the very first day we met. We were both English majors. As a result, we had many of the same classes and circle of friends. We started to hang out together, study together and discuss our plans after college. When our fall semester was over, Wayne asked if I wanted to spend the winter break with him and his family in New York. I'm ashamed to admit it because I grew up only hours away from the most famous city in the world, I had never been to New York. The closest I had come to New York was Trenton, New York. I feel embarrassed just say that. When Wayne made the offer, I did not hesitate to accept. Just thinking about being in the *"Big Apple"* over the holidays was more excitement than I could stand.

We left Petersburg and caught the Amtrak train to Grand Central Station. As we stepped off the train, I had the song *"Living for the City"* by Stevie Wonder playing in my head. In the song, the main character is amazed by the size and beaty of New York. I thought I was ready. Being from Philly, I'm used to the big city; however, Philly is no New York as I soon came to realize. New York City was overwhelming. There were people everywhere. I soon found out that people in New York do not walk; they run. My head was spinning because of the peace. Wayne saw the excitement in my eyes and decided to take me on a tour of some the major landmarks. Our first stop was Madison Square Garden. I had seen "the garden" on TV, but never in person. We next traveled down 5th avenue, to Central Park. New York had everything: theaters, shops, and skyscrapers-the city was huge. After our sightseeing, Wayne informed me it was time to catch the train from Manhattan to Brooklyn. I have ridden on subways all my life, but a New York train ride is a unique experience. The subway cars were filthy, crowded, and there were aggressive homeless people everywhere. In addition, some of the people looked so strange; I could not help but stare. Wayne gave me the protocol on riding the subway in New York-only one rule-do not look at anybody no matter what they are doing. He said, *"Look at your feet until you get to your stop."*

The ride was long, but we finally made it to Brooklyn. Wayne lived in a quiet neighborhood with beautiful trees and manicured lawns. As we neared his house, he briefly told me about his girlfriend. She was Jamaican and attended NYU (New York University). He told me that tonight we were going to meet up with his girlfriend in Queens and that after meeting up with her, we were going to a Jamaican nightclub. Ya Mon! After being introduced to Wayne's parents, we ate, relaxed, and then prepared for our evening out. Wayne's girlfriend met us at the club. She was thin, but extremely attractive. To my surprise, at the Jamaican night club, the food is a major part of the club experience. There was beef jerky, curry rice and beans everywhere. As soon as we walked through the door, I could hear Peter Tosh. Blasting in the background. Heavy steel drums vibrated in my ears. After filling my stomach, I went out to the dance floor and attempted to move with the music. As I mentioned earlier, I can't dance. Therefore, I am sure I looked foolish, but I was having too much fun to care. Once, again, my HBCU had exposed me to an aspect of a culture that I only saw on TV. I can recall similar experiences with college friends on road trips to Washington, D.C. visiting Howard, Baltimore visiting Morgan State, Richmond visiting Virginia Union, but to me New York City was the most memorial trip. All my new experiences connected me to Black friends who attended HBCU's and was the impetus for me forming meaningful and lasting relationships. Gia Vonni, a 2013 Hampton University graduate said, *"I loved the people, the atmosphere, the events, but most importantly the unity we as young African Americans have had together. I would encourage young black brothers and sister to consider attending and HBCU as well, simply because it helps you remember who you are and where you come from."*

TRANSFORMATION

"It is not our differences that divide us. It is our inability to recognize, accept, and celebrate those differences."

Audre Lorde

Why I chose an HBCU…?

Spike Lee, Director (, *Do the Right Thing, School Daze, Malcolm X, BlackKKlansman & Da 5 Bloods*)
Morehouse College

My father went to Morehouse, my grandfather went to Morehouse, my mother went to Spelman, and my grandmother went to Spelman. I took a class at Clark with my film professor Dr. Eichelberger, who is still there teaching at Clark AU. He's the one that really said that I should try to pursue filmmaking. *School Daze*, very simply, is my four years at Morehouse and the impact of the homecoming weekend. The good, the bad, and the ugly. I remember the man directing the coronation my senior year and that was a big success that left me with confidence. Those coronations at Morehouse, they're like Broadway productions!

Not just Morehouse, but I think Black colleges are very essential to our education of young Black minds. Being Black in this country

is never going to get old. There's an understanding, a nurturing at HBCU's that you might not get elsewhere.

In the fall of my third year at Virginia State, a life-altering event happened to me; I became a Muslim. Let me give you a little context, during my junior year in high school, my father had converted to Islam. My parents had recently divorced and my brother, sister and I staying in the family house with my mother. Due to the contentious nature of the divorce, the co-parenting situation was one-sided. The father who had been a stable and fixture of my childhood now had to make an appointment to see his kids. When he could visit, he had to wait on the porch outside the house. That is where the visits took place. I am sure his reluctance to pay regular child support and my mother's struggle to pay the household bills played a role in his forced exile from the family dwelling. In a divorce situation, children are the ultimate victims, always caught in the middle of adult drama. Black colleges sometimes fill the parental void that cripple many young Black boys and girls who face such hardships. This was my situation and Virginia State University once again was my salvation.

With my sister away at college, my dad would frequently take my brother and me to the temple (religious place of worship) to listen to sermons about Black empowerment, civic responsibility, and cleaning up one's so that they could be a service to humanity. We would hear the same statement every week from the minister. He would say, *"Allah's (God) mission is to lead a people lost in the wilderness of North America."* At the time, neither the sermons nor the strict lifestyle impacted me or my brother enough for us to convert. My mind was not receptive to the message even though I could see how the religion had profoundly changed my father. Through my formative years, my had become increasing self-destructive, self-absorbed, and narcissistic. These are not qualities conductive to be a good husband or father. When he accepted Islam, he did a 360. The way he talked, dressed, and carried himself was totally different from the man I had grown to love even despite his imperfections. He had abandoned most of his vices and was now driven to be self-reflective and committed to the uplift of African Americans. I have been around many people who have had their Paul moment. In the Christian tradition, St. Paul was knocked off his horse by a blinding light and gave up complete control of his life to fellow God's plan, that was my father minus the horse. Few of those people maintained their transformation for the duration of their lives and kept that level of commitment until their death. My dad was exception. He became my spiritual example on how deep faith can change any man regardless of their personal failings. One of the great disappointments in my life is that upon my father's death, I never let him know what a profound religious impact he had on my life and how proud of was of the man he had become.

After attending summer school at the end of my sophomore year, I ran across a friend, Wayne, who had spent the summer overseas and coincidently had converted to the religion of Islam. On the surface, this may not seem like an unusual occurrence, but because of my mindset at the time, I was now receptive to accepting a new direction in my life. To my surprise, I was not alone. One of my closet college friends, James, was also open to the possibility of choosing a new path in his life. Prior to Wayne's conversion, my core group of friends were all on a collective path towards self-destruction. Religion was an aspect of our lives that we were all missing. Collectively, our grades at Virginia State were horrible and our lives lacked both meaning and purpose. At the time, getting a quality HBCU education and taking advantage of the opportunity we were provided was not on our minds. We viewed college as an extended vacation; and going to classes increasingly became a rarity. At the time, my friends were from the north and due to that fact, we had all been exposed to elements of Islam. The religion had already infiltrated many of the African American neighborhoods in Philadelphia, New Jersey, and New York. In the early 80's the religion of Islam, had not yet spread in any substantial way to Virginia.

Our friend Wayne had the nickname *"Worm"* and his name was indicative of both his personality and mannerisms. You meet the most interesting people at HBCU's. Worm was the type of person who could light up a room. He was outspoken and people gravitated around him. He always had some type of scheme that he was working on. Most of his schemes were legal, but just barely. When he accepted the disciplined orthodox version of Islam, we were all shocked, but we knew if Worm was sincere, Islam could also provide the change we needed in our own lives.

Wayne quickly informed us that he had gone to the City of Petersburg's Court House and legally changed his name. He informed us that he now went by the name Hudaifah and that Islam had changed his life giving him meaning and purpose, and that it would do the same for all of us. He made this proclamation to a group of his friends, me included, in front of Jones Dining Hall. Hudaifah further stated that 'we' should all accept Islam immediately and get our lives right with God. I use the word 'we' because Hudaifah was directly his comments specifically at his friends from the north. He was the type of person that when he involved himself in anything, he put his entire heart and soul into it along with his unique personality. I witnessed my father and ministers from the temple give that same "fire and brimstone" speech, but at that specific time in my life, standing in front of the school cafeteria, my soul was completely exposed. I'm not sure if this was my Paul moment, but I was ready to accept Islam right on the spot. The merging of religion and academia at my HBCU was inevitable because the freedom to be yourself and feel comfortable about your life choices was welcomed and encouraged at Virginia State.

It must have been the way Hudaifah presented his conversion story with such zeal and conviction that finally caught my ear. In addition, the seed that the men and women from the Nation of Islam, like my father, had cultivated; made me, along with my northern friends convert immediately without reservation. I personally was not sure what I was getting into, but the fire was lit. Some people may call it a leap of faith, I would say it was more a last-ditch attempt to save myself from the destructive lifestyle I was leading. Hudaifah taught us the rudimentary elements of faith, the five pillars: Belief in one God, Prayer five times a day, Charity, Fasting, and a Pilgrimage to Mecca once on our lifetime. Everything was happening so fast. The feelings I had were strange, but I knew I needed a change, and this seemed like the perfect time. One of my many blessings is that I was not going through this experience alone. I had my closet college friends walking through this faith journey alongside me and the unwavering support of HBCU family.

Hudaifah told us that we should change our names, the way we dressed, and our overall behavior. This seemed like a tall order, but in unison, we marched to City Hall and submitted our applications to legally change our names. Hudaifah had an Islamic book of names, and we all went through the process of reinventing ourselves. As I proceeded to select a new name, I wondered how I was going to explain the name change and conversion to my mother. I wondered if she would feel betrayed that I was abandoning the faith of Christianity that she had raised me in and instead follow the religious path of my father. My siblings and I attended Taylor Baptist Church in North Philadelphia during my adolescence. This was a requirement of my mother. As a family, we went every Sunday, and I occasionally Sunday school. Fortunately, I had underestimated my mother. She was so understanding and accepting of the fact that I was attempting to transform my life and become a better person. And student. I love her so much for allowing me to make my transition and supporting my decision from the very beginning. On a side note, my mother is a devout Christian. She was a member of a Black congregation in Norfolk, Virginia. She was listening to a sermon one Sunday when the pastor during a sermon negatively portrayed Muslims and the religion of Islam. My mother went to the pastor after the sermon and told him she had a son who was Muslim and that what he said about the religion of Islam in general and what he said about Muslims specifically was inaccurate. The pastor listened but would not denounce his words to my mother or to the congregation. My mother told him where he could go, in a few choice words and relinquished her membership on the spot. She had been a local and devout member of the church for ten years. That's my mom!

People never fail to amaze me. The reaction I received during my transformation from Dr. Wyatt was heartwarming. He was both my English professor and academic advisor. Dr. Wyatt was the first person to fully embrace my new faith. He saw my transformation as a type of personal pilgrimage and was more than willing to support his advisee who was making a positive change in his life. He was not the only professor on campus that took a keen interest in me, but he was the one who took my transformation personally. We would sit for hours discussing my conversion. As an academic, he was always intellectually curious. I love this about smart people. Dr. Wyatt took it as a personal challenge to learn as much as possible about Islam to help me on my journey. As a Christian, Dr. Wyatt understood clearly that anyone trying to find their spiritual path to God should be encouraged, even if that path is different from the one you chose. His connection to me during this critical time in my life was invaluable. I try to take this approach when I meet people of other faiths. My job is to be kind, compassionate, and accepting of anyone trying to get closer to his or her Lord. This personal relationship with your professor is typical at HBCU's and one of the main reasons that Blacks who attend these colleges and universities remain loyal to their schools the rest of their lives.

During heated discussions, Dr. Wyatt would enjoy picking my brain. He would ask me pointed questions about Islam and would challenge me to draw comparisons between other monotheistic faiths. He helped me understand the continuum of Judaism's connection to Christianity, Christianity's connection to Islam and Islam's connection to these two great religions. I never knew they were interrelated until Dr. Wyatt put me through these religious tutorials. We would converse on the merits of the Quran (Islamic holy book) and compare it with verses commonly recited from the New Testament. He would routinely debate me on my knowledge about Islam so when I was questioned about my faith, I knew what I was talking about. Keep in mind, Dr. Wyatt cared about me. This was not apart of his job description as my academic advisor.

He was just an elder allowing a young man searching for meaning in his life, to find himself. This meant the world me.

Hudaifah's light continued to burn brightly for my remaining two years at Virginia State. Our growing community routinely studied together both about Islam and our academic subjects. We had daily tutorial sessions to focus our attention on the purity of minds, bodies, and soul as it related to our new faith. These sessions allowed us to avoid the pull of outside influences on campus. As a result, collectively our grades improved and our commitment to spiritual growth became crystallized. Without Islam, the support of my new circle of coverts, and Dr. Wyatt I believe deeply that I would still be marred with self-doubt and mediocrity and would not proudly hold a degree from Virginia State University today. The communal experience of brotherhood that I encountered from both faculty and students at my HBCU left an indelible mark on my development and made me into the man I am today.

CONCLUSION

"Education is that whole system of human training within and without the school house walls, which molds and develops men."

W.E.B. DuBois

The transformative power of Virginia State University has shaped and developed this wayward soul and made him into a man with character, integrity, and intellect. My four years on this majestic campus have made me so appreciative of the blessings that God has bestowed on me, a young Black man searching for a meaningful life. Those burning questions that one asks when at a crossroads in life, such as: Why am I here? What is my purpose? How can I contribute? What truly gives my life meaning? These questions and so many more were answered for me at my HBCU. The real education that you receive at college is not the academics. The more important lesson is independence, the ability to act and think reflectively. The accumulation of knowledge should be the cornerstone and the development of creating the full person. The individual who confidently presents themselves to society equipped with the tools acquired to make a real difference in the world. Virginia State University has supremely outfitted me with this armor.

After taking a few years after graduation to find out how I could best use the tools I received from Virginia State University, I decided to become a teacher. Armed with a B.A. in English, I started my career at Sister Clara Muhammad School in Philadelphia. This small Islamic School afforded me the opportunity to develop my craft while placing me in an environment of like-minded people. The experience was life affirming. Helping to shape young minds and feeling that my calling nurtured at Virginia State University was being put to good use has been gratifying. In loving memory of my supportive wife, Denise, and my three amazing daughters Jahaan, Khadijah, and Maryam, I was able to return to school and receive two masters degrees and a doctoral degree to better prepare me to be a more skilled educator. After thirty years in the field of education, I have taught at private, charter, and public facilities, taking on the role of classroom teacher on the elementary, middle, and high school levels. For the past ten years, I have been an adjunct professor at Norfolk State University, an HBCU in Norfolk, Virginia.

As I transition into a new chapter in my life, published author, I have had time to reflect. One of the great thinkers of the 20th century, W.E.B. DuBois said, *"Education is that whole system of human training within and without the schoolhouse walls, which molds and develops men."* These words struck me because Virginia State University, like so many HBCU's, became the training ground that took a boy and turned him into a man. It provided academic rigor support, guidance, and constant encouragement. I love and value my HBCU, and I pray that in some small way you learn to love and value them, too. The culmination of all the stories you have just read, along with my personal narrative illustrate both the value and need for HBCU's. These great institutions of higher learning were originally founded on the premise of giving equal educational opportunities to African Americans. For all the graduates who have been blessed to receive an HBCU education, we realize that the experience has been transformative. Please continue to support HBCU's because a people who do not have a link to their past will always be lost.

BIBLIOGRAPHY

Bultrymowicz, Sarah. *Historically black colleges increasing serve white students.* http://time.com/2907332/historically-black-colleges-increasingly-serve-white-students (accessed June 27, 2014)

Carter, Kelly. 18 *celebrities on their hbcu days* https://www.buzzfeed.com/kelley/carter/18-celebrities-on-their-hbcu-days? (accessed September 4, 2016)

Gasman, Marybeth. *Changing Face HBCUS.* www.gse.upenn.edu/pdf/cmsi/Changing_Face_____HBCUS.pdf. (accessed April 12, 2016)

Kaufman, Michael. *Stokely Carmichael, Civil Rights Leader Who Coined 'Black Power' Dies 57.* www.nytimes.com/1998/11/16/us/stokely-carmichael-civil-rights-leader-who-coined-black-power-dies-at-57.html (accessed June 10, 2017)

Lomax, Michael. *Churches played vital role in historically black college's success.* www.cnn.com/2010/opinion/09/19/lomax.uncf.black.churches/index.html (accessed May 11, 2017)

Merch, Dana. *Amazing Facts HBCUS* https://www.linkedin.com/pulse/2-amazing-facts-hbcus-Dana-i-merch-mpa. (accessed June 10, 2017)

National Center for Education Statistics. *Annual Reports Program.* https://ncse.ed.gov/pubsearch/pubsinfo.asp. (accessed May 8, 2016)

Quinlan, Casey. *5 Things that make it hard to be a black student at a mostly white college.* https://thinkprogress.org/5-things-that-make-it-hard-to-be-a-black-student-at-a-mostly-white-college (accessed January 25, 2016)

http://onlineblacklist/net/10-quick-facts-on-hbcus-that-you-might-want-to-know (accessed September 4, 2016)

Printed in the United States
By Bookmasters